Mollie Jean Goes to Her First Soccer Practice

Michael Barr

Dedication

Mollie Jean Goes to her First Soccer Practice is dedicated to my mom Jean. As the oldest of eleven children, my mom was always there for each of us. Looking back, I still cannot understand how she shared her love with all of us.

Acknowledgment

I would not be the successful coach I am without the guidance of three wonderful friends and role models. Chris Jones, Bob Urban and Lew Atkinson. They were instrumental, assisting and guiding me at different times of my coaching career.

About the Author

Michael Barr is well known in the soccer world. He has received numerous awards from the United States Soccer community as well as hall of fame status in high school, college and the state of Pennsylvania. He has been a featured speaker and instructor at United Soccer Coaches Conventions. He has written numerous articles on coaching soccer as the Director of Coaching for Eastern Pennsylvania for 18 years.

In addition to coaching soccer, he was a special education teacher working with students from elementary school through high school.

Michael and his wife Barbara have four wonderful children and nine grand children.

My Dad asked me in the winter, "Mollie, would you like to play soccer?"

I said, "OK, Daddy, let's go."

My Daddy said, "Not so fast, soccer star. We don't begin until the spring, but we have to get you signed up for soccer now."

Finally, all the snow melted, and soccer practice was in a few more days.

My Mom and Dad took me to buy my first soccer ball. My Mommy said, "Mollie, a size three soccer ball is for little girls like you. Bigger boys and girls play with size four or size five soccer balls."

 It was the perfect size for me. I couldn't wait for soccer practice.

The day finally came. From my car seat, I could see little boys and girls on a big field with plastic disks of every color, balls, and little soccer goals. I knew this must be where I practice. My Mommy walks me to a man with big legs and a big smile.

"Hi Mollie, I'm Coach Chris. Welcome to soccer practice. I am so glad to meet you."

I held my soccer ball close to me with my hands, though I knew from watching my older brother, my sister, and my uncles I was not supposed to use my hands when I played soccer.

Some of the other kids standing next to me were bigger than I was, and some were smaller. It seemed soccer was for every little girl or boy.

Coach Chris said to all of us, "Boys and girls, look at me. I can do something fun with the soccer ball, can you?"

Coach Chris said, "I can touch the ball with the sole of my foot. Where is the sole of your foot?"

Many of us touched the bottom of our shoes. One of the boys even fell over.

"I can touch the ball with the sole of my left foot. Does everyone know which foot is their left foot?"

I couldn't remember which foot was my left, but Coach Chris showed me. Now, I was sure my other foot was my right.

Coach Chris told us to move the ball with our feet. "This is called dribbling," he said.

Coach Chris asked us to touch the ball with our knees, elbows, head, laces, inside our foot, outside our foot, and finally our backside as we dribbled the soccer ball. We all laughed as many of us fell when we tried to sit on our ball.

Coach Chris said, "Hens should never roll off their eggs. They will never hatch."

Coach Chris waited until we all stopped laughing and said in a loud voice, "Animals like to play soccer, too. Guess what animal I am?"

Coach Chris bent at his waist and placed the ball on the back of his neck, but somehow, the ball didn't move.

"What animal do I look like?" Coach Chris asked.

I raised my hand and said, "You look like a camel with a hump on your back."

Coach Chris said, "Very good, Mollie. Can all of you show me a camel with your soccer ball?"

We tried to balance the ball on the back of our necks, but only a few of us could do it without our hands.

"Animals play soccer too! Can anyone show me how another animal may look when they play soccer?" asked Coach Chris with a big smile as he walked between all of us.

A boy named Albert, who took swimming lessons with me, said, "Guess what animal I am?"

Albert had put the soccer ball in the palms of his hands and swung his arms back and forth.

I thought he looked like an elephant, but before I could guess, Marissa said, "You are an elephant."

Albert said, "You are right."

We all walked around as elephants, pretending we had the ball in our elephant trunks.

Coach Chris said, "Animal children love soccer as much as human children. Show me another animal that plays soccer."

Coach Chris recognized a little girl next to me and asked, "Amy, what animal can you show me?"

Amy looked up to the sky with her finger on her chin and placed her ball on the ground. She lay on her belly, with her head near the ball, and began to push the ball with her head.

Amy said, "I am a snake." Amy made a hissing sound as she pushed the ball with her head.

Coach Chris said, "Let me see all of you become snakes."

Our T-shirts became dirty, but we didn't notice because we were all laughing so hard.

Thomas, a little boy I knew from pre-school, raised his hand and said to Coach Chris, "What animal am I?"

He held the ball in one hand and scratched the top of his head while he made a face by pushing out his bottom lip with his tongue. We looked at each other, but we were unsure of what animal Thomas could be.

Coach Chris looked around and saw a tall girl with red hair raising her hand.

"Yes, Kellie?" asked Coach Chris.

"I think Thomas is a monkey," said Kellie.

Thomas shook his head up and down in agreement. We all became monkeys, making monkey sounds.

"Any other animals who may like to play soccer?" asked Coach Chris.

I raised my hand and showed him my favorite animal. I had put the ball between my two feet and moved the ball slowly with both my feet pointing out. I had also put my hands by my sides with my fingers pointing out.

Gio, who lived on my street, shouted out, "You are a penguin."

I smiled and said, "Yes," real loud.

"All right boys and girls, let me see you pretend to be all the animals we've seen play soccer," said Coach Chris.

All of us became soccer-playing animals. We made noises and bumped into each other and laughed really hard.

Coach Chris suddenly said, "Animals freeze!" Nobody moved until Coach Chris said, "I think my soccer animals need a drink, even the camels."

We all ran to our water bottles. The mommies and daddies on the side of the field were all smiling. I saw Coach Chris moving the cones around in our practice space.

After our break, he called us out and asked, "Can anyone guess what I made with the orange discs?"

I couldn't decide what he made, and the other boys and girls were also unsure.

Finally, Coach Chris said, "It's a pirate ship, and I am the captain."

Suddenly, he pulled a pirate hat from behind his back and put a patch on one eye.

"All of you are my crew, and when I say swab the deck, you have to dribble your soccer balls all around the ship to get this ship clean. Don't go outside the cones because you may fall in the ocean. Since you are my crew, every time I give a command, you have to say, 'Aye, aye, Captain Chris.' Does my crew understand?"

We shake our heads up and down, but Coach Chris reminds us to say, "Aye, aye, captain."

"Swab the deck," shouted our Captain Chris.

We all said, "Aye, aye, Captain Chris," and began to dribble our balls all around the deck.

"Faster!" shouted Captain Chris.

We all said, "Aye, aye, Captain Chris," and we moved faster with the balls at our feet, careful not to dribble off the boat into the ocean.

Suddenly, Captain Chris shouted, "Sharks off the side of the ship, kick your balls as hard as you can into the ocean to scare off the sharks. Try to kick your balls with your laces."

We all said, "Aye, aye, Captain!" and we kicked our balls into the ocean outside the cones.

"You saved our ship, congratulations! I think my mates deserve another water break. Gather up your balls and get a drink."

I was really thirsty and glad my mom filled my water bottle to the very top. As I drank, I watched Coach Chris on the field setting up small goals on both ends of a rectangle he made with the plastic orange discs. He brought out his bag to the side of the discs and had every ball in his bag.

"Boys and girls, this is your soccer field. The lines of discs next to the goals are called the end lines, and the other lines are called touch lines. When the ball goes across the lines, a new ball will come onto the field. You don't have to chase the ball. Now line up, shoulder-to-shoulder, and face me."

He touched the first player in line. Gio, he said, "You're on the Pirate team."

Amy was next, and he said she was on the animal team.

He went down the line until we were all put on either the pirate team or the animal team. I was with the animals. Then, Coach Chris had three animals standing in front of one goal, and three pirates stood in front of the other. Coach Chris asked all of the animal team if they knew what goal they would be shooting toward. We all pointed to the goal behind the pirates. He also asked the pirates the same question, all pointing to the goal behind my team, the animals.

Coach Chris reminded all of us, "Every time the ball goes in the goal, across the touchline, or over the end line, a new ball will be kicked in by me. Do you know why, because I am King of the Soccer Balls!"

He reached into his bag, pulled out a cardboard crown with little soccer balls all around it, and placed it on his head. He kicked the first ball toward the pirates, and most of us didn't know what to do. Thomas, who played for the pirates, received the ball, dribbled all the way down, and kicked the ball into our net.

Coach Chris shouted, "Thomas scores for the pirates!"

Coach Chris suddenly kicked the ball toward my team, the animals, but Amy kicked it over the touchline. Suddenly, a new ball came from the king, but this ball was bouncing in the middle. Kellie ran to the ball, but it hit her knee, went into the air, and landed next to my feet. I kicked the ball as hard as I could with my laces on my right foot, and the ball began to roll toward the goal and slowly rolled into the back of the net.

"Mollie scores a goal for the animal team!" Coach Chris said in a loud voice.

6
5

The balls seemed to last forever, and I really thought Coach Chris was doing some magic because there seemed to be plenty of balls, and he never ran out of the balls. I finally realized Coach Chris had the moms and dads chasing the balls that go over the touchlines or end lines, and they brought them back to him.

"That's funny," I thought to myself. But then he was King of the Soccer Balls, so he could get them to do whatever he wanted! Of course, the parents were having as much fun as we were.

Finally, Coach Chris said, "That's the game, boys and girls. Each of you get a disc and bring it to me as fast as you can and then find your ball and give it to your mom or dad and get a drink of water."

Coach Chris called us out for the last time and told us he had never seen better players.

He pointed to all of us and said, "Mommies and Daddies, How about a big hand for our future soccer stars?"

All the parents had big smiles as they clapped their hands.

Later that night, my Daddy tucked me into my bed. He kissed me on my cheek and said, "Sweet dreams, Mollie."

That night, my dream was all about a soccer game on a field surrounded by a colorful jungle. I was playing with all kinds of animals and friendly pirates, and every player was smiling and laughing, even the animals. I dribbled under a camel and scored. A friendly pirate gave me a "High five."

A monkey on my team said, "Good goal, Mollie."

I looked toward the touchline and saw Coach Chris with his soccer crown on his head, smiling and giving me a "thumbs up" with a huge smile on his face. I could hardly wait for my next soccer practice.